THE REMINISCENCES OF
William T. Smoot

INTERVIEWED BY
Dr. John T. Mason

U.S. Naval Institute • Annapolis, Maryland

Copyright © 1996

Preface

Most of the oral histories in the Naval Institute collection deal with the active service of career naval personnel. William T. Smoot spent only four years on active duty, and this memoir covers only one operation from one tour of duty. But it is a powerful one, because Mr. Smoot had an unusual vantage point during the abortive Bay of Pigs invasion of April 1961. In April 1973 he shared his recollections with Dr. John T. Mason, then the Naval Institute's director of oral history, in a candid interview. During his lifetime, Mr. Smoot declined to authorize the release of the interview. Fortunately, his brother Robert, acting in his capacity as personal representative for William Smoot, has now agreed to make the interview available.

In the completion of this volume, I have done some slight editing in the interests of smoothness and clarity. Ms. Ann Hassinger of the Naval Institute's history division has made a significant contribution through her diligence in the overall process of printing, proofreading, and overseeing the binding.

Paul Stillwell
Director, History Division
U.S. Naval Institute
August 1996

WILLIAM TRUMBO SMOOT

Born: 2 May 1937
Died: 4 April 1994

Education:
  Baltimore city public schools, grades 1-6
  McDonogh School, grades 7-12, graduated June 1955
  U.S. Naval Academy, graduated June 1959
  University of Maryland Law School, 1965-66
  Loyola College Business School, 1968

Active Duty, U.S. Navy: June 1959-May 1963
  USS Eaton (DDE-510): electronics material officer, antisubmarine warfare officer, weapons officer. Participated in hunter-killer exercises with Task Group Alfa and two unmanned space capsule recoveries.
  Destroyer Division 282, staff operations officer
  Destroyer Squadron 32, staff operations officer
  Cruiser Force, Atlantic Fleet, aide and flag lieutenant
  Cruiser-Destroyer Flotilla 12, aide and flag lieutenant

Naval Reserve billets:
  Naval Reserve Surface Division 5-4, division officer, assistant training officer, training officer, 1963-67
  Reserve Destroyer Division, Fifth Naval District, staff operations officer, 1967-68
  Naval Reserve Surface Division 5-1, operations officer, training officer, 1968-70
  Naval Reserve Group 5-1, program administration, 1970-71
  Inshore Undersea Warfare Division 5-3, operations officer, executive officer, commanding officer, 1971-74
  Coastal River Squadron Two, executive officer, 1974-75
  Readiness Commander Baltimore, program coordinator, 1975-76
  Voluntary Training Unit 206, 1976-81
  Active duty for training, 1964-81, various assignments

Civilian Career:
  Assistant corporate secretary, Black & Decker Manufacturing Company, 1963-69
  Vice president and partner, Alex. Brown & Sons (stock brokerage firm), 1969-94

Authorization

The U.S. Naval Institute is hereby authorized to make available to individuals, libraries, and other repositories of its choosing the transcript of the late William T. Smoot's oral history interview concerning the Bay of Pigs. The interview was recorded on 4 April 1973 in collaboration with Dr. John T. Mason, Jr., for the U.S. Naval Institute.

The undersigned does hereby release and assign to the U.S. Naval Institute all right, title, restrictions, and interest in the interview. The copyright in both the oral and transcribed versions shall be the sole property of the U.S. Naval Institute. The tape recording of the interview is and will remain the property of the U.S. Naval Institute.

Signed and sealed this ___9th___ day of ___July___ 1996.

_____ Personal Representative
Robert Smoot
for the estate of William T. Smoot

William T. Smoot - 1

Interview with Mr. William T. Smoot

Place: U.S. Naval Institute, Annapolis, Maryland

Date: Wednesday, 4 April 1973

Interviewer: John T. Mason, Jr.

Q: It certainly is pleasant indeed to meet you, Mr. Smoot. You are kind to wish to record your story, your part in the Bay of Pigs episode, for the future use of historians, whenever it becomes available for that kind of use.*

Would you begin, sir, by telling me something about your background? You were in the Navy. What rank did you hold and something of that sort?

Mr. Smoot: I'll go back. I'm a native Marylander. I went to the Naval Academy, and I was a graduate of the class of 1959. I went to sea from the academy and spent a little over four years on active service; I left the service in 1963. I'm still in the reserves. I left active duty as a lieutenant and am now a lieutenant commander in the Naval Reserve program in Baltimore in inshore undersea warfare.

Q: Actually, you're an active member of the reserve.

Mr. Smoot: Yes, ready reserve is what I am. I have been in the reserves since the time I left active duty and hope to be a true, real reservist as long as that's available to reserves.†

My experience as far as active duty goes, I was first on the USS Eaton, which was a

---

* In mid-April 1961 a force of 1,400 Cuban exiles, secretly trained by U.S. personnel in Guatemala, landed in the Bay of Pigs, on the southwestern coast of Cuba, in an attempt to overthrow Fidel Castro, that nation's Communist dictator. The invasion attempt was a disaster. President John Kennedy decided that U.S. naval intervention would worsen the situation, so ships and aircraft offshore were prohibited from taking part in hostilities.
† Mr. Smoot eventually reached the rank of captain in the Naval Reserve.

DDE, a classification which I believe is phased out.*

Q: Yes, I think so.

Mr. Smoot: These were actually <u>Fletcher</u>-class destroyers, short-hulled, non-FRAM'd ships, and this is the ship that I was on initially during the Bay of Pigs operation.† This ship and at least one other ship that I know of from that division, which was DesDiv 282 out of Norfolk, participated.‡ The other ship was the USS <u>Murray</u>, DDE-576, which was a sister ship to the <u>Eaton</u>. We were home-ported in Norfolk and had been doing, up to that time, ASW hunter-killer work with a carrier.§

Q: Was this under Admiral Ward?**

Mr. Smoot: We were under several admirals. I believe at the time that we left the hunter-killer operations it was Admiral Ailes, Red Ailes.†† We had several in sequence, and I'm not really sure. We were taken out of that op group, as I recall, the first of April in 1961.

---

* USS <u>Eaton</u> (DD-510) was commissioned 4 December 1942. She had a standard displacement of 2,050 tons, was 376 feet long, and 40 feet in the beam. Her top speed was 36 knots. She was armed with five 5-inch guns, ten 40-millimeter and seven 20-millimeter guns, and ten 21-inch torpedo tubes. She was decommissioned 21 June 1946, reclassified DDE-510 on 2 January 1951 and recommissioned 11 December 1951.

† FRAM--an acronym for the fleet rehabilitation and modernization program. Under this program many U.S. destroyer-type ships of the 1950s and 1960s were substantially modernized by extensive rebuilding that incorporated later technology than that available at the time of original construction.

‡ DesDiv--destroyer division.

§ ASW--antisubmarine warfare.

** Vice Admiral Alfred G. Ward, USN, was involved in the Cuban Missile Crisis when he commanded the Second Fleet from October 1962 to August 1963. However, at the time of the Bay of Pigs operation he was on duty in the OpNav staff in Washington, D.C. Admiral Ward's oral history is in the Naval Institute collection.

†† Rear Admiral John W. Ailes, USN.

William T. Smoot - 3

Q: When did you first have knowledge of the fact that you were going to be involved in this particular operation?

Mr. Smoot: We were never told exactly what the operation was to be. In fact, I don't believe that any men on the ship, including the officers, knew that we were even going to the Caribbean. We were a desdiv flagship.* The commodore, the captain, and the exec, in retrospect, appear to be the only people who had a reasonably full knowledge of what the ship was to do.†

Our first intimation that the ship was going to be involved in any way was when we received special radio equipment, which was covered and was used only by the captain, the commodore, or the exec. There were special charts, which were covered, and the exec did all the navigating. No one else was allowed to see them.

Q: How much in advance was that?

Mr. Smoot: I would say these things came aboard the first week of April. Another peculiar thing, we also received two doctors on board, which was unusual for a destroyer.

Q: That must have made you a bit apprehensive!

Mr. Smoot: Right. We had a division doctor who floated from ship to ship, but to have two on one ship was unusual, and this created a great deal of speculation. We were told we were leaving for two weeks, which had been our normal schedule--out two weeks, in two weeks. Our general exercise area had been the Virginia Capes and a little father north, up as far as Newport.

---

* The Eaton was the flagship for Captain Robert R. Crutchfield, USN, Commander Destroyer Division 282 in 1960-61.
† "Commodore" was the honorary title for Captain Crutchfield as division commander. The commanding officer, "captain," of the Eaton was Commander Peter R. Perkins, USN. "Exec" refers to the ship's executive officer.

We left Norfolk--some of the dates are a little hazy, having been 12 years ago--about the tenth, the night of the tenth of April, and headed south. Of course, it's not hard for sailors to tell which direction they're going. We headed south, and shortly after we left port--I would say two days--on a nice day we lay to, put scaffolds over the sides, scaffolds around the stacks. We painted out our hull numbers, painted out our stack insignia, painted out the name on the stern. We painted out all identifying marks on the ship.

Q: Did you have any guests on board at that point?

Mr. Smoot: No, we had just our regular crew plus the two doctors.

Then, after we'd painted everything out, we proceeded farther south. On our way out of Norfolk we had passed the Boxer, the old non-canted-deck carrier.[*] She had deck-loaded light planes of the observation type, commercial type, Cessnas or whatever. I happened to notice, having been an OD during that period of time, that she stayed within radar range of us all the time.[†] We each got charts of our own and plotted where we were going, and obviously we were headed almost due south.

A day or so later we passed Key West, and I had just come back from Key West. I was supposed to have been in sonar school at the time there. We passed close enough to Key West to see the buildings, in the distance the mirage effect where it looks like the buildings and the sun are floating on the water. After we passed Key West, we headed southwest, almost due west. The day after we passed Key West, I had the deck, and it was about dusk, about 2000. The commodore came up and said to me, "Keep a sharp radar lookout. We anticipate picking up seven contacts, and they'll be together."

Q: Still no explanation?

---

[*] The Boxer (LPH-4) was in 1961 an amphibious assault ship, having previously been an attack carrier and then an antisubmarine carrier. Actually, however, Mr. Smoot may have been mistaken in his recollection. The aircraft carrier that operated in support of the Bay of Pigs operation was the Essex (CVS-9), originally a sister ship of the Boxer.
[†] OD--officer of the deck.

Mr. Smoot: Still no explanation. So about an hour and a half later, I picked up seven small radar contacts and called the commodore and called the captain. They came up, and the commodore said to the captain, "There they are." I asked who they were, and he said, well, these were people that we were going to stay within visual range of during the night. We would open at first light to radar range, and we were not to be within visual range during daylight. So when I was relieved at midnight, I gave these instructions to my relief and went down to my cabin. I got a call from the commodore: would I please come up to his cabin.

I went up to his cabin, and he explained to me that these were seven merchant ships that we would be, he said, "shepherding" for the next day or two. We were never to be within visual range during the day and were never to lose them on radar at night. He said that we were going to Cuba. I just assumed at the time that we were going to take these seven ships or boats or whatever they were to Cuba, and that would be it.

Q: You weren't cognizant of radio reports ahead then extant on mysterious training in Guatemala or anything?

Mr. Smoot: Yes, we had, because I had read in--I think it was The New York Times-- about training camps in Guatemala and also in Florida.

That night--and that would have been the 15th, I think--I had another night watch. I had the midwatch, having had the previous watch the night before.* I got up to go on watch, and, as I usually did, I went to the wardroom for a cup of coffee. There was a sentry there, and he said, "I'm sorry, sir, you can't go in the wardroom."

"Why not?"

He said, "The captain's orders are that no one goes in the wardroom." By then, of course, all of these things had started to fit together.

---

* On board a Navy ship the midwatch typically runs from 2345 at night to 0345 in the morning.

In the old Fletcher class, I don't know if you recall, you could go down below the main deck, forward through the chiefs' quarters, come up through the magazine to the forward mount and into a void that was right forward of the wardroom. There was a door between the forward void and the wardroom in the first level of the superstructure. I went up there, and the door there was unlocked. I opened it, and I could see, lying on the wardroom table, a man with a hole in him about half the size of his abdomen. One doctor was operating on him with the assistance of a corpsman and another sailor. Lying on one of the settees in the wardroom was another man who had his heel shot away.

I immediately closed the door and went up to the bridge. When I went up to relieve the watch, the commodore was on the bridge, and he said to me, "Have you been in the wardroom?"

I said, "Yes, sir."

He said, "Then you see we've had an accident."

I said, "Well, sir, these people weren't on our ship."

He said, "They came on while you were sleeping. We closed one of these merchant vessels and took these two injured men off."

I looked out, and we were very close to about four small merchant freighter-type ships. We were going very slowly. It was explained to me that these men had been practicing with a .50-caliber machine gun on one of these merchant ships.[*] It hadn't been securely fastened down, so it came loose and injured these men.

In the meantime, there appeared on our after deck a gray fiberglass boat with an outboard motor. I grew up right here on the Chesapeake Bay, up on the Magothy River, and I was curious. After I got off watch that night, I went down and looked at it. It was an Evinrude motor with a special housing with a lot of insulation on it, which I assumed made it very quiet.

I had breakfast, and the commodore called me up again. He also called up another officer on board, our operations officer. This fellow was married to a Cuban girl, and she was at that time visiting her parents in Cuba. He called the two of us in and said, "We may

---

[*] The gun mishap was on board the merchant ship Atlantico.

have a job for you two to do tomorrow. I'll let you know when, and I'll let you know what."

I said, "Obviously we're going to invade someplace." He said yes, and it would be at first light the next day, which would be the 17th. So we stayed up all night, and what happened was that these seven merchant ships started straggling all over the place.

Q: They were old jobs.

Mr. Smoot: They were very old rust buckets. In the meantime, we had been talking to these people on these special radios. It appeared to me from my limited Spanish--actually, at least three of the skippers were Greek, but occasionally an American would be speaking regular, ordinary, American-type English on the radio. We picked up before first light, which would have been the night of the 16th, four Cuban voices and one American, who was called Gray. That was not his name; he just went by Gray.* He was a middle-aged man who wore glasses and seemed to be in charge of these four Cuban boys.

Q: And they came from one of the merchant ships?

Mr. Smoot: They came from one of the merchant ships, and they came over in another boat. I still remember them; when I get into the story you'll see why I remember them. Two of them were named Carlos, and we called them Carlos Number One and Carlos Number Two, because we couldn't keep their last names straight. They are subsequently living in Miami. Another one was Blas Casares, who was from Camaguey in Cuba, and he's living in Hialeah.† His father had been a cattle rancher in Camaguey and had his ranch taken away by the revolution. These boys had been trained, two of them in Florida and two of them in Guatemala, and they called themselves the Cuban UDT.‡ They later informally

---

* "Gray" was the alias for agent Grayston Lynch of the Central Intelligence Agency.
† Hialeah is a city in southeast Florida, about five miles northwest of Miami.
‡ UDT--underwater demolition team.

made me an honorary member of the Cuban UDT and gave me that as a memento of the occasion.

Q: "For country and for freedom."

Mr. Smoot: Yes. I said, "What is your part in this?"

They said, "We're going to go in before the rest of the invasion."

I said, "How many people are you taking in?"

They said, "Approximately 2,500, but they're coming from different places, and we don't know what the actual total is."

This was getting very close to first light, and we had moved in to within, I would say, two miles of the shore. We were also within visual contact of lights on what I worked out to be the Murray, which was the other ship. Also, we still had this radar contact, which I had surmised to still be the Boxer.

The invasion started after first light, and we moved in even closer. Right at the Bay of Pigs there are several sets of breakers. There are evidently reefs at graduated distances from the shore, and we moved in to the point where we could just look off the ship and see white water. I had my own pair of binoculars, and I was sitting on top of the pilothouse. Where they came from I don't know, but I believe they were LCUs and LCIs, large, flat amphibious-type vessels, loaded with Cubans.* Each one appeared to have at least one or two Americans on board. These came from or around these seven merchant ships that were all within sight except for one. Then everything seemed to happen at once.

Suddenly there were planes everywhere in the sky over the beach.† There were F8Us--Crusaders, I believe--obviously our planes but with no insignia.‡ They were all painted completely gray. There were old PBYs, there were old B-26s, there were Guatemalan planes. There were other South American countries' planes, and I'm not really

---

* LCU--landing craft utility; LCI--landing craft infantry.
† For a firsthand view of the role of the carrier Essex (CVS-9) in providing aviation support of the Bay of Pigs operations, see William C. Chapman, "A View from PriFly," U.S. Naval Institute Proceedings, October 1992, pages 45-50.
‡ Actually, these were A4D-2 Skyhawks from Attack Squadron 34 in the Essex.

sure exactly which ones, but I did identify the Guatemalan planes. It was like a World War I movie. There were little dogfights in the air, but the F8Us just flew up and down the beach, parallel to the beach, and didn't engage at all in this conflict.*

Q: Where had these planes come from?

Mr. Smoot: They appeared from over the horizon behind us. They also evidently had the same kind of radio gear in the planes that we had in the ship, because we could hear them talking in Spanish.

It was getting very light now, and the landing force had gone in. I could see on the beach there appeared to be one main road that came down to this beach, and the beach is not that big. As you face the Bay of Pigs, it's basically just a funnel-shaped bay. The beach was to our right, to the right of the bay. You know, really it's not a very large beach. My first impression was that this was an awfully small place to have a landing. On the left side of the bay, whose mouth is very wide, but we had come that way so we could see the left side of the bay, were just mangrove swamps, intertwined roots, and a small beach before you got to this small beach area.

Even before the first Cuban expeditionary force members hit the beach, I could see militiamen on the beach. It's not funny, but it was almost a comic opera, because the uniforms were different, and you could tell that some had dark pants and khaki trousers, and some had khaki shirts and some had dark shirts, and some had a patch. The liberation force or the expeditionary force had an identifying patch that was red or a bright color. I would say that only half of the people who started in actually set foot on the beach.

There was a lot of gunfire. I was then in the pilothouse because the commodore had called me down. I was listening to the radio, and an American voice was saying, "Would you please tell [I can't remember the code name; all I can think of is Big Boy] to send the air support down."

---

* For more on the activities of the A4Ds and a detailed account of the overall Bay of Pigs operation, see Peter Wyden, Bay of Pigs: The Untold Story (New York: Simon and Schuster, 1979).

They came back in about 15 minutes and said, "When is the air support coming?"

In the meantime, the commodore was calling someone else. I don't know who it was--had a code name--about the air support. The commodore answered back to whoever it was on the beach who was calling and said that the air support was on its way. It was totally light now. I don't know what time it was. About five or ten minutes later the people on the beach called and said, "We need the air support now."

The commodore called whoever it was he talked to, and they said, "We will advise you when the air support is coming."

There were several more transmissions, and finally the voice on the beach said, "If you don't send the air support within the next ten minutes, all is lost."

The commodore made one last call, and whoever it was he was talking to said, "There will be no air support."

He had to call the beach and say, "There will be no air support." There followed profanity from the people on the beach. We could hear gunfire on the radio, and that was the last we heard from anyone on the beach.

In the meantime two of these--I think they were LCIs or LCUs propelled by giant diesel outboards--had come over to our ship, and we were about 100 yards off. These were people who never made it ashore.

Q: This was fortunate for them, was it not?

Mr. Smoot: Well, they were very disheartened. By this time we could see at least two or three tanks on this road that led right to the beach. There appeared to be only one road. Something else had come up. There is an airstrip back from the beach. You cannot see it from the beach. And the plan was to take this airstrip and land these small planes on this airstrip. One of these tramp steamers, for lack of a better term, was carrying aviation fuel, and he took off in the opposite direction when things started going badly. We called him and told him to turn back, and he wouldn't. So we sent the <u>Murray</u> to get him back, and he had to threaten a shot across the bow and various other things to get him to come back. I suppose if I were a mercenary and I were carrying a deck load of aviation fuel, I don't think

I'd have been too anxious to stay around, but he did come back. We allowed him to leave in about another hour when it was obvious that the battle was going poorly and was pretty much a disaster and we wouldn't be able to take the airstrip.

In the meantime two planes had been shot down, and the Murray had picked up one of the pilots. The pilot was a Czech. He was flying some unknown air force's airplane, and he was transferred over the side. They also picked up another pilot, and nobody has ever been sure, but he appeared to be Chinese. He was dead when they found him. He had been ejected, parachuted, and the oriental pilot evidently had crashed with the plane but had gotten out of the plane and drowned. The Murray kept these bodies, and I don't know to whom he delivered them. I think they were taken to Vieques.[*]

This was mid-afternoon now, and very few people were left on the beach. The commodore ordered the two destroyers back out of the firing range for the tanks, I assume, although I don't know what a tank's range is.

Q: Was there any attempt by the Castro planes to attack the destroyers?[†]

Mr. Smoot: No, none whatsoever.

We left the beach area, and we towed two of these amphibious craft, which were really outboard-powered barges. We were towing very slowly obviously, because it's difficult to tow a string of barges behind a destroyer. At supper time one of the Americans on one of the barges closest to the ship called and said he hadn't eaten since that morning. He asked if we could give them something to eat and some water, which we did.

We went all the way to within horizon distance, I suppose, to a mile off of the beach. The Murray called and said that they had picked up several of these barges with people on board, and they had also picked up several more of these gray fiberglass

---

[*] Vieques is an island off the east coast of Puerto Rico.
[†] Fidel Castro led a successful revolt against the regime of Fulgencio Battista in the late 1950s. Castro became Prime Minister of Cuba on 16 February 1959 and subsequently President of the country on 3 December 1976. The Bay of Pigs operation was an unsuccesful attempt to oust Castro from power.

runabouts. We, in the meantime, had also picked up two that had floated out. No one was in them. There were just the outboards floating around, and we picked them up.

We stopped, and we took these barges alongside and gave them food and water. Some of the people were very sunburned and didn't have hats. We gave them things to wear that we had. We really weren't quite sure what to do with them. We called whoever the commodore was talking to and asked that we should be relieved of the burden of these barges. That night, after dark, an APA appeared and took the barges from us. They also took some people from the barges who were ill and that we had taken aboard previously. The APA looked like the Cambria to me. I spent a midshipman cruise in the Cambria, and this looked very much like it, but I'm just guessing. Many of those ships looked alike, especially the APAs.

I hadn't eaten since breakfast, and I went down to the wardroom to get something to eat. As soon as I sat down, the commodore called me again, and he called Dick Kauffman up to his cabin.* He said, "I have a job for you two."

Q: Dick Kauffman was the other chap he said this to previously?

Mr. Smoot: He said, "I want you to take the whaleboat and a rubber raft, and I want you to go into the swampy side of the Bay of Pigs and pick up as many people as you can get into a rubber raft and a whaleboat."

Q: Now, this was approaching the night of the 17th?

Mr. Smoot: Yes, this was the night of the 17th. We said, "Who are we looking for, and who do we want?"

He said, "I'm going to send one of these Cuban UDT boys with you." Well, in the meantime the Cuban UDT boys had gone in and come back; three of them had come back. The fourth one did not come back, and Gray did not come back.

---

* Lieutenant (junior grade) Richard Kauffman, USN.

We said, "Are we supposed to be armed?"

He said, "Yes, I want one man in the boat to take a rifle, and I want each of you to take a .45, and I don't want you to get out of the boat. In those circumstances I don't want you to bring anything back except people, and under no circumstances are you to leave the boat."

I don't know if you've ever taken a whaleboat through breakers.

Q: No.

Mr. Smoot: Well, it's a difficult thing to do. It was a double-ender, which made it a little easier, but when you're towing a rubber raft it's a little hard. We went through one set of breakers, actually had a sort of a grounding, just a touching, then deep water again. We came into a second set of breakers, and then it sort of flattened out into almost what you would visualize as a shallow lagoon right up to the beach, where just small waves lapped on the beach.

It was dark, totally dark. There was no moon, and my impression was that it was pitch black. We took a signalman, we took a radioman, and we took a bowhook, and there were two of us in the whaleboat. We were given a password which, in retrospect, seems absurd, but it was "John sent me."

Q: By the way, do you speak Spanish?

Mr. Smoot: I speak no Spanish whatsoever. I speak French and a little Italian, and that's about all. Dick Kauffman speaks Spanish very fluently.

We went in, and we decided that the only way to find somebody was to turn a light on. We had battle lamps which we turned off and on in no particular sequence. The noise from this small surf was enough to block any voice that you could hear, so we weren't able to distinguish human sounds. Dick and I decided that if we were going to find anybody we had to get out of the boat and go on the beach, which we did. The first person we found was an old Cuban fellow lying half in the water and half on the beach. He just was absolutely petrified when he saw us and started to gibber in Spanish. Dick said that he thought we were militia. We were dressed in old wash khakis without insignia, tennis shoes, and no hats.

Dick explained to him that we were friends and that we were going to take care of him. He had been shot in his thigh and wasn't able to walk. We carried him to the boat, which meantime was paralleling the beach, grounding about every 200 feet. This fellow turned out to have been a sergeant in Batista's army.[*] He was very loyal to the old regime and very much against Castro. I would say he was 65, maybe older. We asked him if he knew where any other people were. Incidentally, he was stark naked. He did not have one stitch of clothing on. His feet had started to swell. Later, when we got him back to the ship, his feet looked like two melons. This had come from running through the swampy area in bare feet and cutting his feet on the roots of these trees. He had opened up wounds, and there already had been some infection.

He said that the group of men he'd been with had gone back into the jungle, into the swamp. Dick and I decided that it wouldn't be too wise for both of us to go back in there, since we really weren't supposed to be there at all. We rationalized that being on the beach was really not being on the island, because the beach was wet, and we were still in the water.

We asked this fellow the name of his outfit, and he told Dick in Spanish. Dick wandered up and down the beach calling. Finally one man came out, two men came out, three men came out, five people came out. They recognized us as Americans, and in this group was Gray.

Q: Who was an American.

---

[*] In the mid-1930s Fulgencio Batista, a sergeant in the Cuban Army, had led a successful revolt against the regime then in power. He himself became head of the country and ruled essentially as a dictator until ousted by Castro's forces in 1959.

Mr. Smoot: Who was an American--CIA, I assume. We asked him where the rest were, and he said that most of them had actually been swimming across the bay, from the side on which the beach is located to the opposite side.

That night we found two more. That made a total of seven, plus this old sergeant. Felix was his name.

It was early in the morning now, and we were supposed to be back before it got light. So we put these people in the boat and in the rubber raft, and we went back. We just headed right out to sea and headed . . .

Q: Did you have any difficulty getting over the shoals with a load on board?

Mr. Smoot: No. Strangely enough, as we went farther down the beach, the water got deeper. We found this out, so the next time we came in, we went farther up the beach.

Q: Were these men in bad condition too?

Mr. Smoot: No, these men were in pretty decent shape. It's interesting to note that Dick and I picked up a total of about 17 people over the next several nights. These people were trained in different camps, and we picked up several people who were stark naked. Later the doctor explained to me that--I'm not a psychologist--this is a fairly common thing in a state of abject panic and great fear. When you want to get away and you're being pursued, mentally you want to get rid of every impediment to your speed. This is something that is a reasonably common happening--just get rid of everything that you think is holding you down. They had no shoes; they didn't even have underclothes on.

Other people we found had taken their shoes off, tied them with their laces around their waists, had saved something to put on their heads. You could tell a very strong difference in training at the various camps at which these people we trained. As it turned out later, these people were from different camps. The ones who were well-prepared were from a particular camp, and the ones who weren't were from another camp.

Q: Isn't that interesting? It underscores the need for proper training for any enterprise.

Mr. Smoot: We went back to the ship, took these people back. Many of them hadn't had food or water for a day, a day and a half, or two days. Several of them had been drinking salt water.

Q: Again, a lack of proper training.

Mr. Smoot: Yes. This happened as we got further away from the day of the landing. More and more people turned out to have been drinking it.

Q: You mean on your second expedition?

Mr. Smoot: Yes. We went back to the ship and then went back the next night. We went in only at night, and we were supposed to be back at the ship at first light.

Q: Were you able to rest in the interim?

Mr. Smoot: Yes, but it's very difficult to sleep when you're all keyed up like that.

The third night we went in, and we broke the rudder on the whaleboat going in. We broke it before we got very close to the beach, so we took the rubber raft the rest of the way and told the boat crew to wait for us. They had orders to rig a jury-rig rudder. We went in, and I think we found two people the third night. They were both in pretty bad shape, and we had to carry them. Then we couldn't find the whaleboat. It became light.

Q: And the destroyer was standing off how far?

Mr. Smoot: Well, it was out of visual range. They came in at night and then went out in the daytime.

William T. Smoot - 17

By this time it was light, and Dick and I decided that we would have to go into the swamp to get out of sight. So we went into the swamp, and we hadn't gotten into this dense growth five minutes when a helicopter came over just at tree level height, and there was a militiaman in it. It was an old helicopter like we used in the very early ASW days. It had a side door rather than the belly hatch. There was a militiaman lying on his stomach, firing a rifle down into the jungle. This indicated to us that there were more people around that we hadn't been able to find.

We went farther back in, and we found a little clearing where there was a big Coca-Cola syrup can and some things that obviously had been recently tossed there. We found one more man who came out into the clearing.

Q: The clearing was a dangerous spot at that point, wasn't it?

Mr. Smoot: Well, when I say "clearing," it was a dry spot, maybe 12 feet square, but the trees were pretty much interlaced overhead. But it was a bright sunny day, and we just stayed there until it got dark, then went down to the beach. My watch had stopped, but I assume it was about 11:00 o'clock, and we saw a flashing light. We had carried the rubber raft into the jungle; it was a small raft. We put these people in. There were too many people for the raft, and it was taking water, so I'd bail and Dick would paddle; then he'd bail and I would paddle. We finally got to the whaleboat, and they picked us up. We went back out to the ship and explained to the commodore what had happened. He said that that was our last night.

The ship went back out, I'd say, 10 to 12 miles off the coast, and we were dead in the water, just lying there. Suddenly, 200 yards off our starboard beam a submarine surfaced. We sent a boat over to the sub. The submarine brought back another man that I am assuming was a CIA man, but he was in the custody of an officer from the submarine, and he was wearing a straitjacket. That sounds a little bizarre, but it was a jury-rigged straitjacket so he couldn't move his arms. He was taken aboard and locked in an officer's stateroom. He was an American. That was the last we saw of him.

Q: What about Gray? Where had he gone?

Mr. Smoot: He was sleeping in my room. He didn't eat in the wardroom; he ate in the room, and he didn't say anything. He'd lost his glasses, and evidently he had to have his glasses. He was practically unable to navigate the passageways without his glasses.

Q: I can appreciate that.

Mr. Smoot: He said he had lost his glasses when he first went ashore, climbing down into the whaleboat, so what good he was I really don't know. Gray knew this fellow who was brought over from the submarine, but the relationship is not clear to me.

We received orders from somebody to take the Eaton into the Bay of Pigs, and that night we took it. We had no choice in the Bay of Pigs. We stuck to the center. We went right on up the Bay of Pigs until we were churning up mud.

Q: And what was the mission to be?

Mr. Smoot: I don't know what the reason was, but we went way up into the funnel-shaped bay, as far as we could go. Those old ships did not have bow-mounted sonar, so actually we were right up to the point where our bow was practically in the mud. We got up there, and it was beginning to get light. When I say "light," I mean just the first streaks of dawn. Then suddenly, out of nowhere, a shell whistled and splashed right by the starboard side of the ship, and then another one and another one. Then one went over and splashed on the port side. I know enough about ordnance to know that once they've bracketed you, you're not in good shape.

Q: They'd got your range.

Mr. Smoot: Right. So the commodore said, "Captain [Unclear], fast, fast." The captain had wanted to leave as soon as we got up there, but the commodore was looking around. We were being fired on by tanks. We were that close to shore, and the tanks were on this road. Evidently this road parallels the eastern shore of the Bay of Pigs. It's in the jungle, and you can't see the road, but it's not too far back, and it leads along the bay, right down to the beach. It's only a one-lane road. You can't pass on it, from what I could figure out.

We got turned around, with a great deal of backing and filling and churning up of mud. Having been at battle stations since the time we started up, we were all buttoned up. There were no hits on the ship, and we took off out of that bay. It was now morning. The next day we rendezvoused with this APA, whatever it was.

Q: What was this, about the 20th?

Mr. Smoot: This would have been, I would say, the 21st.

Q: The whole thing was over by then?

Mr. Smoot: Yes. We transferred everybody that we had: survivors, CIA, if they were in fact CIA, wounded people, and one of the doctors to this ship. I talked to some of these people who came over from the ship to pick these people up, and they said they were taking all these people to Vieques and leaving them there.

Q: Are there hospital facilities at Vieques?

Mr. Smoot: I don't know. The only thing I know about Vieques is that we used to fire there. It was a firing range, and we'd have gunnery practice, at least on one side.

Q: I didn't know there were any installations.

Mr. Smoot: The Marine Corps evidently had some kind of installation there.

On the 22nd we started back to the States. The commodore made an announcement over the ship's 1MC that it was obvious that everything we'd done was the highest order of secrecy, and nothing could be said to wives, family, or other military people.* The only story that was to be told was that we had gone out into the VaCapes for operations and that we were coming back.† We got back in a day before our normal two-week time was up. It takes a lot of moving to get back up to Norfolk in that period of time.

The amazing thing to me is that most of the sailors seem to have been highly impressed with the scheme and didn't tell anyone. Who knows? But the whole thing was kept very quiet. The commodore went off to Washington, I assume, as did the CO of the ship.‡ I went over to the <u>Murray</u> and compared notes with their people. They had done the same thing we had done, and we didn't know that they had picked up, I guess, 15 to 20 survivors.

Q: Just two men involved in the operation there too?

Mr. Smoot: Yes, as far as I could tell. They had stayed farther off the beach than we had, and as far as I can tell, they went in the night that we were up into the Bay of Pigs. They had sent a boat in to the beach. We had been working our way, I guess, to west down the beach farther away from the mouth of the bay, and they had picked up this group of people.

Since that time I have only heard from one of these Cuban UDT types. The commodore is now an admiral. The skipper is a civilian, having retired; so is the exec. Dick Kauffman is not well. Upon my return to the States I was made the commodore's staff operations officer. I'm not sure what the reason behind that was.

---

* 1MC is the designation for a shipboard general announcing system. It features loudspeakers throughout the ship so that all crew members can hear an announcement simultaneously.
† VaCapes--the Navy's operating area at sea off the Virginia Capes.
‡ CO--commanding officer.

There are other things I suppose that I might recall. I can't right now. It would probably be out of sequence. However, they'd be little things that probably would not add to the total story.

Q: Was there any discussion of the change in plans? I understand that the original plans were for landing at a place called Trinidad, rather than the Bay of Pigs, and this is where the Joint Chiefs said you had a 50% chance of success.

Mr. Smoot: I was told by the Cuban UDT boys that they had sent a team of their people with a CIA man to Santiago, which is farther up the coast, east of the Bay of Pigs, to blow up a refinery of some sort. I never was able to ascertain whether they did it or not. They were under the impression that it was done.

They also told me that several B-26s from Guatemala were to drop bombs on Havana and places like that. I read in the newspaper that a plane had dropped a bomb somewhere on the outskirts of Havana; again, whether that's true or not I don't know.

I don't know about any other landing spot other than some people did go to Santiago and the Bay of Pigs. It's my impression that no one else on the ship knew either.

Q: You said that en route you and Kauffman were told that you might have a special mission to perform. As it developed, was this the mission that was intended for you, or was there some other in case it had been a success rather than a failure?

Mr. Smoot: I asked the commodore what we would have done had it been a success, and he said, "That's something you don't have to worry about now."

Q: I guess you didn't, under those circumstances.

Mr. Smoot: I was told by some of the Cuban UDT boys at a later time--this was several months afterwards when I had some contact with this one fellow--that had it been successful they wanted some representation by the American military as having assisted the

Cuban Expeditionary Force. They did not want the CIA to be shown, only military personnel.

Q: Then you'd have had to put on your stripes and be identified.

Mr. Smoot: I don't know.

Q: There is some comment to the effect that if a few things had happened, it could have been a success. I mean, it was a razor's edge kind of thing. Would that be your observation?

Mr. Smoot: In my parochial opinion, had the air support--and I never have known to what extent air support had been promised, but obviously it had been promised. It was expected by the Americans on the beach, it was expected by the Cubans on the beach, it was expected by the naval officers who were running that portion of it on the ships. It's my impression that with air support the least that could have been done would be that the expeditionary force could have taken that airfield. Had they been able to take the airfield and they had planes, they would have been able to go on from there.

I was also under the impression that the planes that would have landed at that airfield would have been non-American planes but foreign countries'. Supposedly this free Cuban expeditionary force was flying, from what I could tell, B-26s; I'm not acquainted with aircraft designations. The F8Us that were flying over the beach, and I really saw only two that were all painted out, were supposedly photo recon planes and were not armed.* I've seen some of the F8Us that were photo recons, and they had two seats and a slightly different cockpit configuration. The planes that I saw over the beach did not have the configuration that the photo recon thing had. Therefore, I assumed that they were armed in some respect. That's a pure supposition on my part.

---

* Again, these were A4D-2s, rather than F8Us.

Q: You said when all these planes suddenly appeared overhead from various places, some of them had the markings of Latin American countries.

Mr. Smoot: The Guatemalans were obvious. The other ones I just was not able to identify, except I know that they were different from the Guatemalan planes. This free Cuban air force, whatever their official designation was, had its own insignia of some sort, but it was not apparent on the planes. It was just a plain olive-drab-looking sort of an airplane.

To get back to the previous question as to whether or not air support would have changed anything, again, I'm not an airedale, but it's my impression there was one road leading down to this beach, and it's very easy to control one road and keep whatever's coming down that road from coming any farther.*

Q: The rest being all swamp?

Mr. Smoot: Right. Now, to the east of that road wasn't all swamp, but thick undergrowth and jungle-like. Evidently it was sort of a resort, this particular beach. It was called Playa Larga. And there were some small cabana-like places back from the beach which you could see through the low growth at the water's edge. Then this airstrip, and I really don't know--it may have been a quarter of a mile back behind the beach.

To me, from an emotional standpoint, this series of calls from the beach for air support became increasingly desperate. The whole thing just was demoralizing, and it was to the men on the ship. They were sailors on watch on the bridge, and they could hear all this. It just spread through the ship, and it was like a tomb in the ship when we pulled away that night.

Q: The cries of dying men, actually.

Mr. Smoot: Yes.

---

* See page 48 of the October 1992 issue of <u>Proceedings</u> for a map showing the position of the airfield relative to the Bay of Pigs.

Q: Doomed men.

Mr. Smoot: Yes. It was a very sad occasion, and a lot of men were very bitter. They wanted to do something, and, of course, we weren't supposed to. Then, suddenly, we weren't even supposed to be involved. These people were very bitter and very sarcastic, and there were a lot of "he who runs away" and this sort of thing. There was a bit of a morale problem until we physically got away from that area and transferred these people who were visual reminders of all the problems that we'd had.

Q: Evidently this was a frustration that you shared with the Chief of Naval Operations as well. He also was overwhelmed by these calls of desperation.[*]

Mr. Smoot: I don't know who our commodore talked to, but I think he was talking to someone in Washington.

Q: Probably the White House. It was supposed to be something that was controlled from the White House.

Mr. Smoot: It was a very, very disappointing thing to us. Later, when the Cuban Missile Crisis came up, I had subsequently been transferred, and I was an aide and flag lieutenant to the admiral who ran the logistics end of the Cuban blockade. We went down to San Juan to run it from there. He was in a small way aware of what had gone on before. I don't know to what extent. But to me that was a bit of a redeeming factor, in that we did show some stick-to-it-iveness in that confrontation involving Cuba.[†]

---

[*] Admiral Arleigh A. Burke, USN, served as Chief of Naval Operations from 17 August 1955 to 1 August 1961. His oral history is in the Naval Institute collection.

[†] In mid-October 1962, U.S. reconnaissance plane photographed a Soviet nuclear missile site in Cuba and the presence of Soviet bombers. On 22 October President John F. Kennedy went on national television to announce a naval quarantine of Cuba, to be implemented on 24 October. On 28 October Premier Nikita Khrushchev of the Soviet Union notified President Kennedy that he was ordering the withdrawal of Soviet bombers and missiles from Cuba.

Q: I'm rather curious. Do you think there's a relationship between the two events? I mean, there was the failure of one and then the threat of the second one.

Mr. Smoot: I could only guess. Second-guessing the President of the United States, I guess, is a very hazardous thing to do. But putting myself in the President's shoes, which, again, is a presumptuous thing to do, I suppose there would be some redeeming value to standing up in the face of something of this sort. Because when you come right down to the bottom line, we were fighting the same thing. We were trying to keep this Communist influence out of Cuba, and during the missile crisis the Communist influence was already there, and we were trying to hold it down. So the horse was already out of the barn, but we were trying to keep the door shut so that the rest of the animals didn't get out.

Q: Somebody told me that one of the fatal flaws in the Bay of Pigs operation had been the assumption that the Cuban populace would rise up immediately and support this effort. This was the Achilles' heel.

Mr. Smoot: These four Cuban UDT boys that I talked to were all from what I suppose we would classify upper-class families. They were all from wealthy families. The father of one was a very large cattle rancher. Another one's father was a doctor, another boy's father had been involved with airlines. They were people of means. I asked Carlos Number One whether or not he felt there would be a popular uprising, and he said only in Havana might you get the popular uprising, because already they had had shortages of food and shortages of shoes and clothing and this sort of thing. Castro had initiated this rather puritanical reign that sometimes happens in revolutions. He felt that the only uprising would come in Havana, which, of course, is basically the heart of Cuba, I suppose, and was not really Castro's bag. His was in the hills and with the peasants, supposedly.

Another contributing factor, in my own personal opinion, was that the United States, whatever arm or branch of it started our association with the Cuban Liberation Front, picked the wrong side, but unfortunately there were no clear-cut choices. There were so many organizations in Miami at that time that to pick one that was the right one would have been an impossibility.

Q: There was no unity in opposition?

Mr. Smoot: There was no unity in opposition. And, strangely enough and as a matter of public knowledge, every one of these groups had within its hierarchy, if you could call it that, spies, for lack of a better word, people who were on Castro's side of the fence. Therefore, there was no element of surprise whatsoever. They were there and waiting when we arrived. To me, if you're going to call off something, you call it off if you know that the element of surprise which was necessary to pull it off is missing. In this case it was missing. It was obvious to everyone that it was missing, yet we went another step toward completion of this operation, almost knowing that we couldn't be successful. I don't think a good military man would have done that.

Q: Admiral Ward told me that all the ammunition for the expedition was housed in one ship, and he said that he didn't think any officer worth his salt in charge of an amphibious operation would do a thing like that. Was it true that it was all in one ship?

Mr. Smoot: This is my understanding of those seven ships, and they were real rust buckets--of these seven ships, I know one had all of the aviation fuel on board. I know that the ship from which we received the two injured men before the invasion, the ones who had been injured by the machine gun breaking loose--I know that that ship carried basically nothing but ammunition. Incidentally, one fellow died. The one who survived was the one who had his heel shot away. He said that all of the machine-gun ammunition and all of the small-arms ammunition were on that ship.

Now, there had been rumors that bombs and various other artillery had been on the ship. I don't know that anyone knows, except the people who loaded the ship and the people who finally unloaded it. As you probably know, two of those ships ended up in Baltimore Harbor, and no one would claim them. The United States Government wouldn't claim them, the Cuban Government wouldn't claim them, and the previous owners from whom they were chartered wouldn't claim them. They sat in Baltimore harbor for, I think, two years.

Q: And then what happened to them?

Mr. Smoot: I don't know. I saw the other day what I believe to be one of the ships still there at one of the abandoned piers. It's listing very heavily, and it's down by the stern, just sort of leaning up against one of the piers. The other ship has gone. I don't know what happened to her. I believe that a scrap dealer made some kind of a deal and towed it away.

Q: Nobody wanted to be tainted by them.

Mr. Smoot: Nobody wanted to be tainted. This appeared in the Baltimore <u>Sun</u>. They had pictures and articles about these ships, because no one would claim them. The story I was told was that they had them leased. I don't think a Greek shipper would just throw away a ship if it has one more crossing in it or one more trip in it.

Q: Not Mr. Onassis, anyway.[*]

Mr. Smoot: No, but my impression is that they'd probably been bought, and no one wanted to claim the purchase. I suppose they used shell corporations and fronts for this sort of thing--a supposition on my part.

Q: Did the commodore ever refer to this episode when you served on his staff later?

Mr. Smoot: Indirectly, yes, most of the time as a matter of saying we don't usually talk about this.

---

[*] Aristotle Onassis, who later married President John F. Kennedy's widow, was a prominent Greek shipping magnate of the period.

Q: Just reiterating the fact that it was still a secret?

Mr. Smoot: Right. He put a lot of himself into it. I thought he was going to die of nervous fatigue, because he went several days without sleep and ate while pacing back and forth. It took a lot out of him--a very fine officer and a fine gentleman. I'd just rather not say who it is right now. He's a rear admiral now.*

His part in it, as far as knowing to whom he was talking, I don't think he knew personally. I think he made some assumptions, and he had been checked out by people in the radio gear he actually operated himself. I think he had some pretty firm ideas, and perhaps sometime it might be interesting to get his side of it too.†

Q: Would you tell me, Bill, that little story about attempting to have some sort of a memento of the episode?

Mr. Smoot: Dick Kauffman and I realized that this was a historic occasion and decided that we would like to have some memento of it. Many of the sailors and other officers had asked me to bring back something from the beach, something tangible. So in the dead of night Dick and I dug up a little palm plant, not a tree but something maybe two feet high. We stashed it in the whaleboat and loaded our pockets with sand.

The last time that we were picked up by the ship, we were being brought on up in the falls. I was sitting in the stern of the whaleboat with this palm plant in my lap. I looked up, and on the port wing of the bridge the commodore was hanging over, and he looked down and saw me sitting there with this palm in my lap. He said, "Mr. Smoot, get rid of that thing immediately." He knew what it was intended for. So I dropped it over the far side of the ship. As I did, I held onto several fronds, and I came up with a handful of fronds

---

* Crutchfield was promoted to rear admiral in November 1971 and retired in that rank in July 1972.
† Admiral Crutchfield was interviewed at considerable length for the book by Peter Wyden, mentioned above. He expressed great frustration at being on the scene but not permitted to lend U.S. support to the anti-Castro Cuban forces.

which I still have, all dried and crackly. And I think I still have some sand in my tennis shoes.

Q: But the poor sailors didn't do as well?

Mr. Smoot: No, I'm afraid it wasn't the five loaves and two fishes. I had only so many palm fronds, and I couldn't give them all out. Dick had some and I had some. That's about the extent of it, although I saved an old pair of tennis shoes for three or four years. The Cuban UDT people told me I had to paint them out, so we painted them black so my white tennis shoes wouldn't show up. I kept these shoes in my closet for years until finally I decided they'd have to go to make room for something usable.

Index To

Reminiscences of

William T. Smoot

A4D Skyhawk
   Operated in support of the Bay of Pigs invasion in April 1961, 8-9, 22

Bay of Pigs, Cuba
   Preparations on board the destroyer Eaton (DDE-510) for support of a planned invasion at the Bay of Pigs in April 1961, 3-8; support role of commercial ships, 4-8, 10-11, 26-27; invasion on 17 April, 8-11; planned air support by U.S. aircraft was not permitted, 9-10, 22-23; rescue of survivors who made their way offshore, 11-12; the Eaton sent two officers ashore in a boat to rescue Cuban survivors, 12-17; the Eaton was bracketed by gunfire from shore when she entered the Bay of Pigs at night, 18-19; relationship between the Bay of Pigs invasion of 1961 and the Cuban Missile Crisis of 1962, 24-25; political aspects of the operation, 25-26; souvenirs of, 28-29

Castro, Fidel
   Cuban prime minister during the ill-fated Bay of Pigs invasion in April 1961, 11, 14, 25, 26

   See also Bay of Pigs, Cuba

Central Intelligence Agency
   Agent Grayston Lynch took part in the ill-fated Bay of Pigs invasion in April 1961, 7, 12, 14-15, 18; a suspected agent was taken aboard the destroyer Eaton (DDE-510) in a straitjacket, 17; CIA men were reported to have blown up a refinery at Santiago, Cuba, as part of the operation, 21

   See also Bay of Pigs, Cuba

Classified Information
   Following the ill-fated Bay of Pigs invasion in April 1961, the commodore of Destroyer Division 282 told the crewmen of the destroyer Eaton (DDE-510) not to discuss what they had just seen, 20

Commercial Ships
   Ships loaded with Cuban troops participated in the ill-fated invasion of the Bay of Pigs, Cuba, in April 1961, 4-8, 10-11, 26-27

Crutchfield, Captain Robert R., USN
   Served as commodore of Destroyer Division 282 during the Bay of Pigs invasion in April 1961, 3-7, 9-10, 12-13, 17, 19-21, 27-28

Cuba
   See Bay of Pigs, Cuba; Cuban Missile Crisis

Cuban Missile Crisis
   Relationship between the Bay of Pigs invasion of 1961 and the Cuban Missile Crisis of 1962, 24-25

Eaton, USS (DDE-510)
   Antisubmarine training exercises in the early 1960s, 2-3; preparations for participation in the Bay of Pigs invasion in April 1961, 3-7; operated in range of merchant ships while approaching Cuba, 4-8; surgery performed in the wardroom on Cubans who had been accidentally shot, 5-6; operations off the coast of Cuba during the invasion, 8-12; dispatched Smoot and another junior officer to go ashore in Cuba to rescue Cuban survivors, 12-17; came under fire while in the Bay of Pigs at night, 18-19; the commodore of Destroyer Division 282 told the ship's crewmen that what they had just seen was classified and should not be discussed, 20; reaction of the crew when the invasion failed, 23-24

Essex, USS (CVS-9)
   Operated in support of the Bay of Pigs invasion in April 1961, 8

Guatemala
   Role in support of the ill-fated Bay of Pigs invasion in April 1961, 5, 7-9, 21, 23

Kauffman, Lieutenant (j.g.) Richard, USN
   While serving in the destroyer Eaton (DDE-510) during the Bay of Pigs invasion in April 1961, was detailed to go ashore in Cuba and look for Cuban survivors from the invasion, 12-17, 28-29

Lynch, Grayston
   CIA agent who took part in the ill-fated Bay of Pigs invasion in April 1961, 7, 12, 14-15, 18

Medical Problems
   Surgery was performed in the wardroom of the destroyer Eaton (DDE-510) on Cubans who had been accidentally shot while practicing for the planned invasion of the Bay of Pigs, Cuba in April 1961, 5-6, 26

Murray, USS (DDE-576)
   Operated in support of the Bay of Pigs invasion in April 1961, 2, 8, 10-12, 20

Perkins, Commander Peter R., USN (USNA, 1945)
   Served as commanding officer of the destroyer Eaton (DDE-510) during the Bay of Pigs invasion in April 1961, 3, 5, 19-20

Rescue on Land
   The destroyer Eaton (DDE-510) sent two officers ashore in a boat to rescue Cuban survivors of the ill-fated Bay of Pigs invasion in April 1961, 12-17

Smoot, William T.
　　Overall summary of his naval service, 1; duty as a crew member of the destroyer Eaton (DDE-510) during the Bay of Pigs invasion in April 1961, 1-29

Underwater Demolition Teams
　　Cuban UDTs supported the ill-fated Bay of Pigs invasion in April 1961, 7-8, 12, 20-22, 25

www.ingramcontent.com/pod-product-compliance
Lightning Source LLC
Chambersburg PA
CBHW080609170426
43209CB00007B/1377